Inson Dubois Wood
Interiors

Inson Dubois Wood
Interiors

Inson Dubois Wood
Foreword by Christopher Hyland
Photography by Mark Roskams
Edited by Daniel Melamud and Cristina Rizzo

Rizzoli
New York
New York · Paris · London · Milan

Contents

Foreword

Christopher Hyland

To be described as eclectic is the greatest accolade for an interior designer. It carries with it an acknowledgment of broad knowledge, acute sensitivity, and recognition of expertise in both the gathering and placement of objects as well as the curating of color—all defining the designer's world, the built world.

Inson Dubois Wood is an eclectic designer par excellence. From the halls of Greenwich, Connecticut's finest houses to Park Avenue, Palm Beach, Thailand, and beyond, clients experience Inson's design exhilaration as he approaches each project with unique, custom solutions. He has design gusto.

A whirlwind of activity inevitably results in rooms that are eminently comfortable yet possess what this writer believes renders Inson's spaces unique: they are cognitive wonderlands, not unlike abstract expressionist paintings. We are challenged to look, examine, and understand the juxtaposition of seemingly different shapes, forms, and colors—as if in a new world. Yet as our senses settle, there is a Zen moment. We pass from the effort of comprehension to the contentment of experience. Few designers challenge us more with better cognitive results.

Inson's work confirms that our culture is alive, capable of integrating the aesthetic narratives of many movements. He gives life to objects by heightening their uniqueness in the context of his design schemes. Yet, even when obviously given boundaries, he excels.

Karl Barth believed that God lurked in Mozart's work. In Inson's work the life of objects—from textiles to furniture and art—is infused with personality, demonstrating that a premier accomplishment of humankind is to both implement and complete artistic expression fully, prominently realized through an eclectic built world, the world of rooms.

Inson Dubois Wood is a design guru.

Preface

Inson Dubois Wood

I was born into a world of design and aspire to inform it as much as it informs me.

As the eldest of seven siblings, my father, Inson Wongsam, rejected his role of inheriting the family business and left his home in northern Thailand to study art in Bangkok. Recognizing his potential, an art professor recommended that he travel to Paris in order to steep himself in the works of Picasso, Brancusi, and Giacometti. As luck would have it, my father won a Lambretta scooter in an art competition in Bangkok. Soon he was on his way to Paris through India, Pakistan, Iraq, Iran, Afghanistan, Turkey, and Greece. Carrying rolled-up canvases in saddle bags, he mounted art shows in all seven countries to support himself along the way.

My mother's family also journeyed west, migrating from France to the United States. After graduating from the University of Connecticut, my mother, Barbara Wood, traveled to Paris to study literature at the Sorbonne. She met my father at an art opening and before long they moved to New York. While my father pursued his art career, my mother became an educator and activist, attending civil rights marches with me in tow. She was an intelligent and indomitable free spirit.

When I was young my parents separated, and my father moved to Manhattan, where he had a small art studio and shop on St. Marks Place in the East Village. He was part of a circle of artists that included Donald Judd, Gordon Matta-Clark, and Isamu Noguchi, and he always encouraged me to view the world through a creative lens.

There was one silver lining to my parents' breakup: each married someone who introduced me to new worlds. My stepfather owned a successful landscape architecture business in Darien, Connecticut. Together, he and I built an elaborate three-story log house with trees we felled and dragged out of the forest. With him I learned that there is no greater reward than building something from the ground up out of natural materials.

During my childhood, I spent much time shuttling back and forth from the white clapboard-sided Colonial homes of Darien to gritty St. Marks Place. Eventually my father returned to Thailand, where he met my stepmother. She was an English expat who had recently divorced her Royal Navy sea-captain husband to pursue her art and Buddhism. This meant trips to Thailand, London, and the liberal-minded English seaside town of Totnes.

My love for residential design is due in part to the importance both my families ascribed to entertaining, celebrating, and fostering community. Whether modest or extravagant, the warm and inviting homes of my youth eventually led to my pursuit of intentional design.

In high school my competitive spirit found a welcome home at Northfield Mount Hermon School in Massachusetts. There I sought athletic and artistic pursuits: flute, painting, and sculpture combined with soccer, cycling, and downhill ski racing. My mother died of cancer during this time and I became emancipated (acting as my own guardian) at age sixteen.

Despite discouragement from my college advisor I applied and was accepted to Cornell's School of Architecture, the nation's most competitive and only Ivy League pre-professional architecture program. Countless all-nighters and a varied curriculum of art history and philosophy led to my winning the fifth-year thesis award in my fourth year for designing an innovative Zen temple. In my last year, I was honored to receive a traveling fellowship to Asia to study Buddhist temple construction as well as the Charles Goodwin Sands Memorial Medal for the top three graduates. My highlight at Cornell was the overseas program in Rome directed by the architectural historian Colin Rowe, author of *The Mathematics of the Ideal Villa and Other Essays.* The program consisted of classes in the Palazzo Massimo alle Terme, analyzing Renaissance architecture, as well as tours of Palladian villas and Roman ruins throughout Italy.

Subsequently I was accepted to Harvard University's Graduate School of Design, where my biggest influences were Rem Koolhaas and Wolf D. Prix, who combined their Harvard studio architecture courses with post-structuralist linguistics and gender studies.

After graduating, I worked at Kume, one of the largest corporate firms in Japan designing vertical cities. When I returned to the United States I collaborated on commercial projects in large corporate settings. Honing my professional skills served as the foundation for my career in residential design.

I transitioned into residential projects when I became design director for Juan Pablo Molyneux with projects in New York, Miami, Canada, Los Angeles, and Paris. Molyneux was often hired for his multicultural perspective; in that respect I fitted right in. Molyneux was also focused on creating opulence—he calls himself a maximalist. Working on houses all over the world, I received a thorough education in traditional decorative arts techniques.

Eventually I accepted an offer from another legendary designer, David Easton. Although a traditionalist, Easton wasn't afraid to mix things up. For example, he'd buy art deco furnishings and use them alongside fine antiques. Both Molyneux and Easton taught me the importance of the designer-client relationship.

With two of the best mentors in the industry behind me, I started my own company. Today, my diverse background and global perspective influence my firm's approach to design.

Beautiful design is a confluence of events. If design is the hub of a project, then builders, relationships, communication, and empathy are all spokes that facilitate it. I owe a debt of gratitude to my clients, contractors, vendors, staff, friends, and especially my family for their support in my continual quest to achieve timeless, aesthetic harmony.

But my goals go beyond design and architecture—I live to share my passions with my clients, and they in turn share theirs with me. It's all about expanding our horizons.

By the Sea

Saint-Tropez

This house, situated on a seaside hilltop just east of Saint-Tropez, was the culmination of a decade's exploration by the owner. The original space was the work of architect François Vieillecroze with interior designers Maurice Savinel and Roland Le Bevillon. The house was meant to feel aged and time-honored: the use of repurposed sections of eighteenth- and nineteenth-century buildings, such as hand-selected cobblestone, antique floors, and recycled doors helped achieve that effect. The project was long in the making. The goal was to tie a variety of periods and locations together in a unified composition that reflected the owners' vision. Our approach involved weaving the elements of the meandering compound, from the main house to the guesthouses to smaller guest rooms, into a tapestry of family memories.

The comfortably worn ambiance unfolds as a three-dimensional collage embracing multiple generations. Bottle and wine jug collections; porcelain and horn cups set out, ready for a shared meal or drinks; miniature figurines; remnants from a fishing trip or remote island exploration; seashells; souvenirs from Morocco, Cambodia, and the Ivory Coast—these pieces all remind us of the mosaic of time and shared experience. The relationship of found objects to their surroundings becomes as important as the objects themselves: an elaborate model sailboat gains gravity and significance when surrounded with artwork by the owners' grandchildren. Treasures well placed throughout the home achieve a balance between arbitrary and intentional, as if to unravel the experience of the home like a good book—page by page, detail by detail, impression by impression.

Design is seamless when the viewer is oblivious to how it came to be, as if it had been there forever—as organic as a hug, the rhythmic breathing of a sleeping lover, or the laughter of a child. The house becomes a dream state, a stream of consciousness where visitors feel the ease of timelessness. The design process fades and we are left with a final question: how did it come to be and where will it take us?

Page 11: An aquamarine indoor-outdoor pool flows through an arched portal. The bifold door slides open on an industrial track to allow for unobstructed views of the garden. A series of wheeled lawn chairs line the edge of the pool and define the garden's perimeter.

Preceding pages: Provence-style orchard and farm baskets arranged at the side of the pool hint at the owners' family tradition of gardening and love of nature, while a carved-stone guardian angel nestled in a niche watches over everyone.

Opposite: An oversized red-fringed tassel drape tie-back restrains an informal screen of beads that rests on the portal leading to the kitchen. A multi-tiered sculptural stone fountain sits above an assemblage of a carpenter's bench and an eighteenth-century Provençal chest of drawers, signaling the path to the conservatory greenhouse.

ATEAU de PIBARNON
TEAU de PIBARNON

Pages 16–17: Found objects from past fishing excursions arranged on open shelves are transformed into meaningful sculptural artifacts. These are mixed in with a butcher's slicer for homemade sandwiches. To the left of the worn metal double doors is a cornucopia of woven baskets, each with a unique shape: one for gardening, fishing, picking fruit, and picnicking.

Preceding pages: Both a vertical and horizontal use of terra-cotta tiles creates a warm backdrop for the open-hearth kitchen's large wood cornice and collection of various-sized glass milk jugs. A patron saint wall fixture blesses the cooking. Between the stone farm sink and butcher's-block table rests a pair of hurricane lamps, and a red ceramic Moroccan tagine—timeless reminders of the past.

Opposite: The continuous motif of stacking layers is seen again with a whimsical wooden hand-carved fish arrangement placed atop a glass jug on a Mannerist wooden étagère.

la Provence de Ducasse

Preceding pages: The ethereal nature of the ceramics displayed in the vitrine contrasts with the abundance of richness embodied in the wooden texture of the doors, ceiling beams, cabinets, and furniture.

Opposite: A pair of free-standing neoclassical wooden columns frames the corridor to the library, where a set of welcoming 1940s Parisian leather club chairs awaits.

An old fishing rope drapes over one of two woven chairs from Aix-en-Provence that surround the wrought iron balcony with stunning views of the Mediterranean.

Opposite: The wooden portal to the main bedroom visually frames a seventeenth-century adjustable reclining chair that is enlivened by an embroidered silk scarf.

Following pages: The multicultural family room captures the spirit of the owner—who is well educated and well traveled—with objects from over twenty countries, including African masks, an Indonesian dragon kite, Moroccan side tables, and an Italian sculptor's block where texture and color rule the day. A coffee table made from an old door displays a collection of horn cups on an antique tray.

LE BÂTON DE PLUTARQUE
L'EMPIRE DES MERS
GEO panoramique

Preceding pages, from left to right: A tranquil simplicity reverberates throughout the home's guest bedroom wing with a variety of distressed wood walls and floors in the bathroom. A large natural sponge is offered up by a ceramic figurine, while a wooden fish acts as an eager voyeur; Hermès Balcon du Guadalquivir teacups on a French carved four-poster bed with embroidered pillows highlight the beauty of hand craftwork.

Opposite: A cantilevered nautical ballast serves as a control lever for the sixteenth-century fortress door, which opens onto a rectangular stone wash basin.

Following pages: A rusted wheeled scupper punctuates the L-shaped pool that interlocks with a series of Palladian structures. The play of light and shadow on the textured wall surfaces echoes the Mediterranean's breathtaking appeal.

Modern Scandinavian

Malmö

This home's owner, a descendant of a notable architect, has design in her DNA. Her art background, strong aesthetic sense, and intuitive painterly eye for light and shadow made for an effortless collaboration.

The pre-existing architecture was clean and modern, requiring a small infusion of warmth to counter its rectilinear glass and metal surfaces. We also wanted to keep things soothing and light given the short Swedish summers and long winters. We assembled an assortment of Swedish antiques and vintage elements into a contemporary mix. The client also wanted a forgiving environment for her children, a place where they could run around barefoot and engage in arts and crafts. Most of the bright colors emanate from well-chosen accessories and the abundance of artwork throughout the home, much of which was already in the owner's collection. The Scandinavian touch of white poplin upholstery mixed with cozy throws and animal furs added neutral tones and texture without drawing the focus away from the art.

In the end, the overall composition reflected the lifestyle of its cultured and well-traveled inhabitants and expressed the sophisticated but modest aesthetic of a city known for its high quality of life.

HOME

INSON DUBOIS WOOD

vanille
Ingefær
basilikum
oliven
AVOCADO
INGEFÆR
PAPAYA
tomat
fennikel
Göteborgs Kex
Göteborgs Kex

Page 39: The outdoor and indoor spaces start to blur as a result of the floor-to-ceiling glass and the pool's reflection. A bronze lantern perches on a wooden Gustavian painted table flanked by mid-century modern chairs.

Pages 40–41: Decorative glass ornaments adorn a dried banyan tree branch placed upright in a massive blown amber vase. Shearling throws provide warmth around a glass wood-burning stove.

Pages 42–43: Eames wire-base side chairs surround a weathered Swedish farm table. An artist's palette becomes a decorative object above a makeshift bar of painted wood.

Preceding pages: A medley of styles flows through the living room, which features a miniature chair collection above the TV cabinet. A Carrara stone and metal Arco lamp by Achille Castiglioni frames a series of butterfly prints, while a contemporary sofa and mid-century modern chair create a dialectic.

Opposite: The modern minimalist kitchen, nearly all white, provides a bright setting for cooking and entertaining. Two nautical-style down lights illuminate the space during long winters.

Above: A vintage slot machine acts as a storage cubby while adding color to the environment.

An abundance of cotton throw pillows creates a welcoming seating area in the outdoor sunroom.

To bee or not to bee!

Opposite: A play of scale, texture, and light defines the garden room display wall, which is made of small seedlings, bulbs, and mosses that provide inspiration for the larger gardens outside. Lavender and cacti are placed in diminutive bowls and miniature ceramic containers. Vintage garden shears and tools serve as decorative objects.

Following pages: The austere modernism of the architecture is softened with the use of vegetation and landscaping. The symmetrically arranged hurricane lamps combined with garden plants along the pool reinforce the sleekness of the existing structure while playing down its rigid lines.

The Red and the Black

Manhattan

I was invited to design two of the most prominent rooms in a prestigious Manhattan holiday show house. The pronounced classical detailing of the existing spaces suggested two alternatives—either complement or contrast. I attempted to do both, looking at my role through a somewhat surrealistic lens.

One of the rooms, organized around the theme of Venice's Carnival, incorporated museum-quality antiques, Rodin sculptures, futuristic furniture, and tailored drapes in a Harlequin print. Adding 1930s Parisian art deco furniture as well as mid-century modern and contemporary elements—such as lighting by Charles Paris, sculptural blown glass by Jeff Zimmerman, and modern art—created a twenty-first-century take on the prewar salon.

From the red-lacquered and gold leaf ceiling adornments that mirror the red-and-white Hermès Balcon du Guadalquivir tableware, to the dining tables by Wendell Castle and custom light fixture by Hervé Van Der Straeten, the room is filled with layers of color and texture. Highly polished ceramic vases and figurines pop against the earthy tones of the original wood paneling.

The second room was loosely based on the Chinese New Year, a vibrant holiday rich with symbolism, cultural heritage, and visual inspiration. At each of the soaring windows, pagoda-shaped pelmets were constructed from a variety of custom fabrics, tassels, and other bits of passementerie. The outer panels of the silk window treatments were matched with the crimson-lacquered wall color, marrying the room's hard and soft elements.

Within the oversized room, I created two separate living spaces: a seating area set off by opposing sofas and a dining area delinked by a pair of mismatched Émile-Jacques Ruhlmann tables. In an attempt to accentuate the room's symmetry, I hung a massive geometric yellow canvas by the minimalist painter Larry Zox opposite a large embroidered silk wall panel of the same color from Fromental. A Jean-Michel Frank buffet table displayed an elegant Jaime Hayon dining set, which held its own against the room's bright colors. A white porcelain Jeff Koons puppy vase on the center coffee table provided a modern and playful focal point, allowing the ornate surroundings to command but never overpower the room's contents.

Page 55: In the grand salon a heavily articulated ceiling with gold-leaf relief and red lacquer highlights a painting by Lloyd Martin, while a Sultanabad rug provides the backdrop for a series of limited-edition ceramic Lladró figurines by Jaime Hayon and a silver tea service from Puiforcat.

Preceding pages: Dining room meets salon with a twentieth-century dramatic black lacquer futurist table by Wendell Castle. A Maison Gerard crystal chandelier by Hervé Van Der Straeten is whimsically placed at the center of the table. Alexander McQueen–inspired window treatments spotlight the windows opposite the mantel overflowing with logs. Above the mantel, Venetian mask molds look down on a massive thirty-foot-long antique Tabriz rug from Doris Leslie Blau.

Opposite: A Carnival-inspired cast bronze bird skull by John Lyle points to the ceiling's reflection, which in turn mirrors the red and white of the Hermès Balcon du Guadalquivir porcelain teapot and plates.

Opposite: In the Chinese New Year–inspired salon, a whimsical tea party is set on an Émile-Jacques Ruhlmann table surrounded by mid-century modern chairs by Finn Juhl. A painting by Michael Dickey is illuminated by a Charles Paris floor lamp.

Above: A Ron Ehrlich painting is suspended below a bronze chandelier by Hervé Van Der Straeten. The grand salon has dramatic tassel-imbued pelmet-style valances with custom curtain trim and walls with hand-embroidered and painted silk wallpaper. A Ruhlmann gold gilt cabinet by Pollaro stands to the right of the yellow Larry Zox painting.

Opposite: To the right of a modernist Larry Zox "diamond" painting sits an ornate 1930s Ruhlmann art deco gilded cabinet. A pair of lamps by Charles Paris is displayed on a Jean-Michel Frank console.

Above: A black-and-white painted floor contrasts with the heavily lacquered crimson red walls.

Following pages: A period mantel is surrounded by a French-inspired zebra chair from J. Robert Scott and a hand-carved chair by Ruhlmann. A pair of Jeff Zimmerman handblown Mercury glass cubes accompanies a blue crystal Rococo table.

Urban Glass House

Manhattan

My clients found a two-family townhouse on New York's Upper East Side that needed extensive work. Designed in the 1920s, its interiors were compartmentalized into confining areas. Our goal was to cultivate a series of open and livable spaces. To maximize the house's perceived width, we created a skeletal stair and cantilevered it off the east wall. The decision not to enclose the stairs with walls gained us almost a foot in interior width. The stair became the focal point of every room it passed through—it is the spine of the home, running from the basement up to the roof, where we added a glass penthouse, whose skylights spill an abundance of sunshine into a six-story light well.

As much of the townhouse's beauty lies in its rear view onto lush garden terraces, we chose expansive floor-to-ceiling glass for the back of the house. We also enlarged the windows on the front facade, making the house feel connected to its location in both directions with sight lines from front to back, allowing natural daylight to flood deep into the home's center.

The color of the architectural materials progressively lightens as one ascends each floor. At the basement level, the stairwell's interior walls are blackened steel and the family room cabinetry is made of ebonized wood. (Even the outdoor garden is paved in black granite.) The living room on the second floor contains a bleached gray Macassar mantel sealed under seven coats of high-gloss lacquer, while the media room is paneled in Wenge, cerused and limed to emphasize its grain. The bedroom suites on the third and fourth levels contain dressing rooms, closets, and wall units made from a variety of pale gray woods. Finally, the children's room and penthouse feature white lacquer built-ins and floors of white milk glass.

The house is a uniform modernist composition that maintains an exacting standard of detail at the micro-level. Lasers were used for tasks that required precision, from aligning structural beams to laying out stone and tile. Many utilitarian features are concealed (the drawers have hidden pulls). Other details are barely visible but serve important roles, like the recessed polished-nickel C-channels at the baseboards that make the walls appear to float. The overall feel is that of complete exposure—with the aperture wide open—as if to say there is no need to display opulence, for it resides within.

Hopper

EXPOSED

Page 67: A steel I-beam facade with floor-to-ceiling glass combined with a glass stair replaced the former masonry facade.

Preceding pages: A red-painted African tribal mask accents a room with silk velvet upholstered hand-carved Italian chairs and a leather and mohair sofa from Promemoria. A Persian contemporary rug by Orley Shabahang complements the contemporary painting.

Opposite: Backlit steel shelves and a lacquered Macassar wall unit surround a custom limestone fireplace mantel.

Above: A Justin Bower painting anchors the open living room. A custom chair covered in off-white Hermès leather with a Christopher Hyland pillow rests on an undyed, all-natural wool rug.

Opposite: Another large painting by Justin Bower is punctuated by a cast bronze lamp with a silk shade.

Following pages: A sculptural cantilevered metal and wood staircase acts as a backdrop to a Romeo Sozzi console table. Hidden glass lights illuminate the stairwell at each level.

IN THE SPIRIT OF SWING

ANTONIO LOPEZ
FASHION, ART, SEX & DISCO
Pucci

Large floor-to-ceiling sliding glass doors flood the kitchen with natural light and open to the rear garden and a glass terrace.

ST. JEAN BAPTISTE SCHOOL

Opposite: A free-standing tub invites a pensive moment to view the sculptural detail of a church across the street.

Above: The bathroom was made of frosted mirrors, white glass, and Calacatta gold marble. A custom monolithic double vanity made entirely of Corian houses a pair of seamless wash basins.

Following pages: The penthouse garden level was created as a simple ode to modern minimalism. Other than a chair and a white-lacquered built-in wall unit, the space is open for exercise.

A Room with a View

Manhattan

In this extensive penthouse renovation, the aim was to create an environment of ease and grace reminiscent of an old-world Parisian artist's atelier. A primary objective was to find ways to highlight the breathtaking fifteenth-floor views of Central Park, with treetops forming the world's most beautiful lawn. Given the client's love of flora and fauna, moments of nature abound throughout: from the dining room mural of a garden forest scene to the floral compositions in the *verre églomisé*–lined dining room cabinets. However, for every surface that's highly decorated, there's another one that's spare, or covered in a simple matte French stucco.

On the apartment's sprawling terrace, we installed a greenhouse that was cast in France entirely in bronze. This, together with enlarged windows facing the south side of Central Park, increased the apartment's natural light.

Knowing that some things are too special to discard, repurposed materials and furniture were used. For example, a bi-level kitchen island was created from two French marble-top consoles, one seventeenth- and one eighteenth-century. We carved a hole into the taller console to accommodate a hammered copper sink and faucet. Boiserie panels repurposed from an eighteenth-century French château line the library walls; an ancient Roman stone basin and spout sits in the powder room; a combination of driftwood slabs and custom glass elements compose the bar; and a rare antique fireplace and mantel from southern France stands at one end of the solarium tea room. The result was an eclectic environment with spectacular pieces bringing layers of history to the high-rise home.

The client, a gardening enthusiast and founder of a New England educational community organization rooted in land stewardship, food, and farming sought a New York apartment where she could entertain and inspire dialogue about food's integral lifestyle role and sustainability. That meant the kitchen had to be inviting, a kind of room-sized cornucopia. Walls came down, allowing us to transform the galley into a large open kitchen. To integrate the kitchen with the rest of the apartment, we avoided upper cabinets and instead used an eighteenth-century armoire-breakfront for storage.

Of course, an open plan requires careful placement of furniture. We created intimate seating areas within the spacious apartment, such as a window seat and a diminutive desk that could accommodate tea for two, and by the use of a Ralph Pucci upholstered lounge chair on wheels. And, for flexibility, we chose pieces that could morph from one thing to another. Notably, the twelve-person hunt table can become a buffet for informal gatherings. Traditional furnishings aside, the spirit of the apartment is innovative and forward looking.

MARC DU PLANTIER
JEAN-MICHEL BASQUIAT
PICASSO SCULPTURE
MoMA

Page 83: Flanked by a pair of 1950s chairs by Dan Johnson, a life-size Victorian cast bronze rooster by T. Comolena sits in an eighteenth-century French mantel with a seventeenth-century Italian guilloche framed mirror featuring original mercury glass.

Pages 84–85: Imported from France, a custom cast bronze and glass conservatory houses an assortment of curiosities including a Victorian iron tricycle with a leather carriage seat and a 1940s Italian parchment veneer box. A Ralph Pucci–upholstered Galileo chair by Patrick Naggar rests beneath a 1940s Italian carved wood lamp. A nineteenth-century German celestial globe by Himmelsglobus is placed alongside a 1920s Parisian lamp. A Robert Lee Morris hammered brass gong punctuates the windowsill.

Preceding pages: A multicolored limited-edition rug from Marc Phillips sets the stage for an eighteenth-century blue Venetian secretary. A 1970s painted red glass cocktail table with a bronze base supports a pair of French brass candelabras. An Altmeyer and Guichard metal parrot sculpture sits watching in the corner.

Opposite: Fortuny silk throw pillows garnish a Ralph Pucci sofa by Elizabeth Garouste in green velvet. An eighteenth-century French painted screen acts as a backdrop and provides a division of space.

Above: A Louis XV bronze *doré* box is surrounded by a set of Swedish champagne glasses by Kosta Boda.

Opposite: A series of cerused and limed Louis XV nineteenth-century boiserie panels from a château outside of Paris line the library walls. An eighteenth-century neoclassical Italian blue-painted gilt armchair sits by an eighteenth-century Irish side table. A pair of Fu dogs surround a French Victorian green and white *pâte-sur-pâte* porcelain bronze box.

Preceding pages: In the dining room a pair of Louis XV rock crystal and gilded bronze candelabras accentuate a seventeenth-century English hunt table surrounded by Louis XIII chairs. A set of nineteenth-century French chandeliers from Carlos de la Puente illuminate the wall mural.

Opposite: A modernist bench from Les Ateliers Courbet sits next to a unique kitchen island made from a seventeenth-century French stone-top buffet and an eighteenth-century Louis XV carved sideboard. A copper-appointed La Cornue range is framed by an antique limestone backsplash and a hand-shaped zinc hood. The repurposed stone floors are made of Vallangis limestone from the Bourgogne region of France.

In the master bedroom, a Napoleonic chaise with carved swans rests on an antique Oushak rug, providing a vantage point for stunning views over Central Park.

Opposite: A pair of eighteenth-century Italian mirrors purchased at Newel, originally from the Hôtel de Longueil in Paris, evokes a pensive stillness. A bronze and marble lamp from Maison Gerard by Achille Salvagni supports a rare ceramic vase from Italy.

Following pages: In the master bedroom, an eighteenth-century English neoclassical table meets with a period French painted wooden bed.

Town and Country

Paris

Located on the Place de la Madeleine, this Parisian loft incorporates the best of two disparate worlds: the urban avant-garde sensibilities of the *Rive Droite* and the rustic charm of an Aix-en-Provence farmhouse. In the City of Light, it was only fitting to embrace the beauty of the surrounding neighborhood, which is imbued with the history of countless creative minds, from Voltaire to Flaubert. The original space recalled an artist's garret ennobled by vaulted ceilings, rough-hewn beams, and wide-plank floors. We incorporated simple, dual-function indoor-outdoor furniture in an eclectic style that encompasses modern and antique sensibilities.

In the living room, a massive tufted sofa provides a perch from which a number of guests can recline on polychromatic throw pillows to ponder the stellar views. Its focal point, a modernist mantel, is gently disrupted by an ethereal indoor garden that feels as if it were plucked directly from the grounds of Eze's Château de la Chèvre d'Or in the South of France. The garden functions as both a significant space in its own right, and as a tantalizing backdrop to the dining area. Modern skylights allow for dramatic rays of light to pierce the interiors. The wallboards create an angular but informal backdrop, at once seductive and casual, conjuring the turn-of-the-century brushstrokes of Matisse in his 1902 painting *A Glimpse of Notre Dame in the Late Afternoon.*

M·SVB·INVOC·M·MAGDALENAE
MOULINS DE PARADIS
ST. FRES

GRAMOPHONE

Page 103: Wicker and natural-edge wood furniture in an indoor-outdoor garden provides for a moment of serenity in the penthouse duplex situated in the heart of Paris's eighth arrondissement.

Pages 104–105: A stripped-down upholstered chair, a driftwood lamp, and an open library filled with instruments and books reflect the owner's diverse interests. A Moroccan rug adds richness to a clean, contemporary sun-filled living room.

Pages 106–107: A low wraparound sofa sectional offers ample viewing of the church at the Place de la Madeleine—a stunning backdrop and historical architectural site in its own right. Nineteen twenties vintage desk lamps impart unobtrusive light while functioning like musical notes against the rhythm of the church columns across the way.

Preceding pages, from left to right: A colorful chandelier made of inverted wine bottles adds a touch of playfulness to the open kitchen and complements the colorful throw pillows on the sofa; a gramophone brings a hint of gravity to the reflections of the original hand-scraped beams and columns.

Opposite: A view to the sun-filled garden room through two beautiful glass doors emerges as an inspiring escape from urban density.

Preceding pages: A massive skylight illuminates the dining table for work or play—the client loves throwing dinner parties. A large circular metal tray acts as a focal point with a Bleus D'Ailleurs Hermès teapot in an otherwise open and airy loft space. A red box-shaded Japanese-inspired floor lamp sets the tone during the evening.

Above: Above the headboard, a book-filled niche with complementary sconces makes for easy reading in bed.

Opposite: Like the bedroom, the walls in the master bathroom are clad with wood providing a durable texture that works well with the natural stone slab vanity.

European Romanticism

Como

With this house there was little need to do more than be a good listener. The building's architectural details embody the essence of European romanticism: aging plaster walls interrupted by old wooden windows—which are rarely symmetrically placed—provide a feeling of enclosure while allowing light to stream inside as freely as shoots in an untended garden. Taking cues from the architecture, I created interiors of playful informality; the window treatments are as mismatched as the windows. This is the kind of house where radiators aren't hidden but used as graphic elements; where bookshelves hug the ceiling as a kind of impromptu cornice; and where a rough-hewn picnic table can work just as well indoors as outdoors.

Because the homeowner is a prodigious collector of art and objects, the challenge was to pick and choose the right combination of pieces. The soothing color palette helped bring the assembled antique furniture and dozens of small treasures from a wide range of backgrounds into harmony. The goal was to create an artful composition, as inviting as the sun-dappled room in Pierre Bonnard's impressionistic 1913 painting *The Dining Room in the Country*. An interior can also be impressionistic—with seemingly disjointed strokes forming a very pleasing picture.

Rotella
Rotella Roma Parigi New York

LA DIVINA COMMEDIA
LA DIVINA COMMEDIA
BOCCACCINO

Page 117: A nineteenth-century Italian turned-leg desk doubles as a console atop a refurbished multicolored terrazzo floor. A modern mirror reflects a framed oil painting across the room.

Pages 118–119, from left to right: Two types of window treatments in the same striped linen gently cover the windows, as poplin slip covers on chairs and sofas prove to be timeless arrangements on a simple sisal rug. A repurposed Italian painted wooden mantel discreetly masks the radiator; a linen-covered chaise longue provides an ideal setting for choosing books in the library, while a large circular floor lamp lights up the ceiling.

Preceding pages, from left to right: A sixteenth-century putto watches over a pair of delicate brazed brass chairs and an exquisitely detailed metal circular table, where doppio espressos are set for two; in the dining area a black metal swing-arm lamp hangs over the table and a late-nineteenth-century Italian drop-leaf folding table acts as a buffet and support for a hand-crafted duck sculpture.

Opposite: A collection of books combined with a swing-arm lamp and an eclectic tabletop display add vibrancy to the breakfast room. The rustic farm table sits below a large translucent linen Roman shade. Scalloped glass bowls and plates speak to the original leaded stained-glass doors, which are accented with a delightful colored rope detail.

A tea set for two waits at the foot of the elevated bed, while a delicate diaphanous tri-part curtain with a continuous valance provides a modicum of privacy; the center panel is elegantly tied back to reveal a work of art.

An eighteenth-century Italian hand-carved fireplace mantel serves as a bookcase when not providing a romantic focal point for a candlelit evening.

A putto nestles in a corner of the garden, watching over those fortunate enough to appreciate his reclined state of repose.

Beach House

The Hamptons

When my client bought a beach house on eastern Long Island, its interiors were like a sketch—a line drawing composed of columns, window mullions, railings, and coffers. The goal was to add the necessary lines to complete the picture. First we applied blue metallic stucco Veneziano to the raised wood panel within the wall paneling, which accentuated the white-painted grid. Then we brought in ebonized furniture with thin, graceful profiles: a large wire-brushed console table holds a pair of oversized Chinese vases in the foyer, and a suite of twelve chairs surrounds the dining table. Above the table, there's another sophisticated doodle: a black and chrome industrial chandelier by David Weeks.

The client didn't want his weekend house, which he bought so he could spend leisure time with his family, to look like every other Hamptons getaway. He wanted to create a home with a hybrid feel—one tied to the past with new-era inhabitants—contrasting the styles of New England cottages with Tribeca-loft chic. The design had to stand up to the thirty-foot ceilings of the living room and correspondingly large windows. We approached the challenge in a unique way by injecting unexpected color, materials, and textures. Nautical and agrarian objects, many found at local antique shops, create a sense of place.

The effects continue beyond the main living area. For the family room, I designed a rug that is an ode to the imagery of pop artists Murakami and Damien Hirst—a sharp departure from the sisal floor covering normally found in beach communities. In the den, a custom-painted surfboard complements the client's art collection. Our work continued outside, where the client might host fifty for a sit-down barbecue. Oversized umbrellas and modern, sculptural wicker furniture punctuated by soothing pastel cushions provide a comfortable and creative setting for relaxed conversation.

Page 131: Perched upon a customized wire-brushed and ebony oak table by Christian Liaigre, a rare set of oversized Chinese Qing-style porcelain vases welcomes guests in the entry foyer.

Preceding pages: A David Weeks chandelier hangs over a dining table surrounded by elegantly shaped Danish mid-century modern chairs. On the upper level, a large basket of branches occupies the corner.

Opposite: A cast bronze cocktail table from Promemoria sits on a custom-designed ink-blot rug, adding a touch of urban chic.

Above: A mid-century modern chair stands next to a wood block print by Thai artist Inson Wongsam on a bleached maple console by BDDW.

Opposite: A Bertoia-inspired vertical multi-shaft candelabra points to a Murakami-influenced custom rug.

Above: A custom Jean Dubuffet–inspired surfboard activates a comfortable family room. An old fishing basket and wooden toolbox hearken to times past.

A cast iron four-poster bed draped with linen faces the contemporary mantel.

Farmhouse on the Mediterranean

Mallorca

This quaint home is located on the outskirts of the ancient Roman town of Andrachium or, as it's known today, Andratx. It is home to descendants of agrarian landowners who maintain the almond, fig, tangerine, and carob orchards, as well as celebrities such as Claudia Schiffer and Guy Hamilton. (The area was the inspiration for Selina Scott's 2009 book, *A Long Walk in the High Hills.*)

The farmhouse, built by the owner's grandfather, contains antique beamed ceilings and terra-cotta floors. The grandfather's self-portrait hangs over the mantel. In furnishing it, one of the goals was to have as little environmental impact as possible, which is why many of the antiques were either family heirlooms or acquired locally. Eighteenth-century chairs and a rustic farm table from a local antiquarian help set the stage in the living room. All the window treatments were done in Mallorcan ikat found in a nearby market. The fabric, a rough cotton linen, was also used for throw pillows, bedspreads, and table cloths. And it was used to re-cover an old George Smith sofa—now the perfect perch for trading anecdotes late into the night. Collectible objects, from seashells to ceramic curiosities, are intentionally displayed.

We approached the project as if we were historical anthropologists mounting an exhibition. For example, old trunks found in storage became side tables and farm hats now serve as a sculptural display alongside impressionist art. The Mediterranean color palette of warm umbers and siennas, muted over time, was inspired by scenic walks through nearby orchards and vineyards. Sunlight dances across the pastel stucco surfaces.

The owner's love of entertaining inspired the selection of an abundance of candelabras needed for dinner parties that continue well past midnight. In the morning, beverages are served in porcelain that, like the guests, comes from a host of countries: German Wallendorf, Austrian Augarten, Spanish Real Fabrica, French Revol, and Italian Cozzi. And coffee may be necessary to shake off the idea that last night's festivities were merely a dream.

Brezo
MATEUS

Page 141: In the foyer an heirloom antique storage chest stands on a terra-cotta tile floor. A pair of old woven farm hats hangs on the wall on either side of a late-nineteenth-century painting of tall ships.

Pages 142–143: In the living room a painting of a boat by the owner's grandfather resides over a pair of eighteenth-century chairs with original tapestry fabric that flanks an Italian chest of drawers.

Preceding pages: The living room is filled with an eclectic array of antiques collected over decades. A portrait by the client's grandfather rests on the fireplace mantel as an old leather trunk transforms into an ottoman for a Spanish armchair. A portrait of the owner as a child is illuminated by a carved lamp with a hand-stitched parchment shade, and a turn-of-the century oak corner vitrine displays a collection of German Meissen porcelain.

Opposite: In the kitchen, ceramic teapots complement modest utilitarian pots and utensils—proof of a family who truly loves to cook and entertain. Portuguese tiles line the edges of the shelves.

Above: Flowers and vegetables from the owner's garden repose in woven baskets. A saffron curtain waits eagerly for a spicy meal to be served in the dining room.

Opposite: A vintage wicker picnic suitcase accentuates an eighteenth-century Italian walnut side table, and a pair of straw hats on a leather trunk recalls times past when vacation travel time was measured in days and weeks, not hours.

Above: Ikat fabrics in blue and red patterns, which are local to the island, are used on window treatments, bedspreads, and pillows. A pair of nineteenth-century French metal candelabra sconces, modified for electricity, illuminates makeshift bedside tables.

An arched doorway with polychromatic ikat curtains leads to one of four outdoor dining terraces.

Uptown Downtown

Manhattan

A group of young millennials founded a social club called Magnises and asked me to design their space. The idea was to make a newly developed townhouse feel established and old world, like a room from Wes Anderson's film *The Royal Tenenbaums*. Because the space was almost exclusively for entertaining and networking, the design had to be functional and durable yet chic and sophisticated.

The process developed organically, as we first focused on meeting a thirty-day deadline for an inaugural event. With a modest budget and aggressive timeline, we designed and constructed built-ins, a walk-in bar, and lounge seating for two floors of the building. Futurist pieces from the Italian furniture-maker Cassina were mixed with everything, from a customized mohair-covered Eames lounge chair to a church pew. Many pieces were found during trips to Housing Works and to a Moroccan import shop on the Lower East Side.

Five types of Venetian plaster combined with polychromatic-painted walls and ceilings became canvases for artworks lent by the illustrious Jane Kahan Gallery. Edgy 3-D computer-generated art by avant-garde female artist Hye Rim Lee adorns the bar and lounge. The launch party included a host of artists, athletes, financiers, and models, setting the stage for the new venture's ongoing success. Our work not only filled the space but established the tone and, like its young founder, portrayed an advanced level of maturity.

F.LEGER
KOONS

KONGSBERG SKI
KONGSBERG SKI

Page 153: A Showtime chair designed by Jaime Hayon rests at the head of a three-hundred-year-old natural-edge Japanese cherry wood slab table by master craftsman Hisao Hanafusa.

Preceding pages: In the upper lounge a wooden coffee table from Cassina pairs with a Moroccan rug, while a Mission-style armchair with original fabric sits next to a 1920s barber's table. A custom mohair-covered Eames lounge chair is flanked by a hammered metal Moroccan side table.

Opposite: A sense of balance reigns in this corner where an African drum used as a side table rests beside a nineteenth-century English glass-front vitrine.

Magritte
Magritte

LEONARDO DA VINCI
ERTE
JACK DANIEL'S

BACARDI

Preceding pages: Computer-generated art by Korean-born artist Hye Rim Lee punctuates a stone and metal table by John Boone. A red eighteenth-century Louis XVI–style shade atop a wrought-iron lamp illuminates a pair of red and yellow Moroccan poufs.

Opposite: A dramatic wall hanging informs the blue walls, yellow ceiling, and red curtains. A modernist hide-covered chair creates a discourse with a French gilded bronze and glass cocktail table.

JOSEF HOFFMANN
LEONARDO DA VINCI

River House

Chiang Mai

This property, nestled against a winding river at the end of a road, evoked childhood memories of Thailand. One was of my father leading us from his home, near Bangkok's original Oriental Hotel, to the floating market, where we selected fresh fish and produce in the early hours of the morning. Another was of riding an elephant in a parade filled with decorative floats and elaborate flower arrangements. These references, coupled with the owner's keen design eye, helped inform the decoration of this unique, open-air Chiang Mai residence.

The main house and a series of guest houses are arranged around a central pool, with water and nature ever present. The owner, Primprow de Gerlache de Gomery, whose guests include academics, financiers, and art world denizens, wanted to create a combination of a gallery, intellectual forum, and social mecca. To assist in this, she had a series of exceptional Asian and Western antiques, artisanal ceramics, and a large number of Buddhas for display.

The building techniques were traditional, with all floors, walls, and ceilings made of solid hand-scraped teakwood, providing a dark canvas for the vibrant art and accessories. The upper level features a collection of traditional musical instruments displayed alongside an antique temple gong. In the sitting room of the master bedroom a vintage Tabriz rug warms the floor and sheer silk panels dress the windows. Lime- and lemon-colored silk pillows adorn a pair of hand-carved teakwood daybeds, from which one looks out over the river for a moment of serene reflection.

THE SACRED SCULPTURE of THAILAND
LANNA STYLE
Lanna Renaissance

Page 163: Two elephant prints guard the entrance doorway to the guest wing. The doors are made from repurposed panels depicting Buddhist figures. A small Ganesha statue, the elephant god of wisdom and new beginnings, watches over the passage.

Preceding pages: Different sized elephants, in a variety of sculptural forms and paintings, are distributed throughout the open-plan living room as symbols of strength and stability. A glass vitrine displays a treasure trove of Thai and European ceramics. Vibrant silk pillows on a pair of antique Chinese wooden chairs define the seating area.

Opposite: A pair of intricately carved doors leads to a sitting room filled with antique Thai musical instruments. These make for wonderful decorative art objects against a sea of hand-polished teakwood wall panels, floors, and ceilings.

Preceding pages: A Colonial-style wicker armchair provides the ideal vantage point to take in an elaborately detailed Thai spirit house sitting on a solid wood coffee table. A plethora of ceramic, bronze, and wooden urns, jugs, and water vessels becomes part of the overall mosaic of the sitting room. Off in the far corner, a Buddha figure elevated on a lacquer cabinet calmly looks inward (while facing outward).

Opposite: A Qing dynasty–style cabinet is the perfect elevated pedestal for an antique bronze Buddha. A reclining Buddha peers back through the looking glass.

Following pages: Silk accents on tablecloths and throw pillows add vibrant color to the open-air lounge that overlooks a winding river.

European Simplicity

Berlin

In the case of this modern apartment on Alexanderplatz in the center of Berlin, the goal was not to overdesign, but to let the interiors reflect the clients' rich European history and culture. Nestled in a quiet side street blocks from chic French and Italian restaurants, the apartment is a pied-à-terre for a family that spends time in New York, Malmö, Munich, and Mallorca.

We created a very relaxed environment that captures some of the flavor of old and new Berlin. Some pieces were inherited from the husband's Hungarian grandparents, who emigrated to the United States—symbols of their voyage include a fabulous collection of vintage leather suitcases and trunks. Other contrasts involve a Biedermeier desk and splashes of modern Italian luxe, such as a footstool by Romeo Sozzi of Promemoria and a pair of leather armchairs found at a nearby weekend market. The interplay of different time periods can be seen in the kitchen, where modern lines are punctuated by a collection of green cut crystal. Anchored by a modern cowhide rug, in the living area a mid-century modern sofa from her native Sweden sits comfortably with an old armchair from his Hungarian forebears. The eclectic collection is a reminder of the historical backdrop that gave rise to the diversity and dynamism of Berlin today.

RTIGIA

MASSERIA

AQUAVIT

everybody must have a fantasy.
the world fascinates me.
art is what you can get away with.

Page 175: A mid-nineteenth-century Biedermeier-style desk doubles as a console table in the entry foyer.

Pages 176–177, from left to right: In the living room, a Bavarian hand-carved wood upholstered armchair sits against a backdrop of light lemon taffeta window treatments. The crocodile and bronze footstool was designed by Romeo Sozzi; the 1930s mismatched leather trunks act as side tables. A contemporary wood and metal cocktail table stands on a cowhide floor covering.

Previous pages: Simplicity defines the eat-in kitchen with a pair of ribbed Murano hand-blown glass bowls that accentuate the dining table.

Opposite: A Thai religious figurine rests on an Italian drop-front desk.

Langenscheidt
Taschenwörterbuch
Schwedisch

Georgian Manor

Greenwich

Finding the right balance of old and new in a classically inspired house is always challenging. The clients commissioned a well-appointed Georgian-style mansion from architect Douglas VanderHorn. Having seen some of my past projects where period styles were intermingled, the clients relied on me to balance the elegance of the past and the comfort of the present. They also wanted the interiors to capture some of the diaphanous qualities of light found in French and Gustavian buildings. As former residents of Germany and Russia, they desired to be surrounded by cultural reminders of their past.

In the same way that King Gustav III brought a pared-down version of Versailles to Sweden, the house attempts to provide a clean interpretation of grand interiors of the past—a relaxed approach to an otherwise stately and formal home. The somewhat formal layout of rooms—sitting room, library, drawing room, solarium—came with one twist: in a rather unconventional move, the wall between the dining room and main living area was removed. We partitioned the space by placing two large glass folding screens with gilded wood frames between the rooms, thus dividing the space without overly obstructing light and views.

Too often the importance of the overall palette and its specific relationship to the art and furniture is overlooked. In the living room, a large monochromatic forest painting by Oleg Vassiliev presides over a pair of unassuming cream George Smith sofas. In the sitting room the color, weave, and texture of the damask I chose for the throw pillows connect the sofa with its surroundings.

Art from the owners' private collection transforms many of the rooms. In the classically paneled aqua Grisaille–painted drawing room, a series of portraits by Sergey Smirnov above the door sets the tone. A modern red painting over the mantel brings a splash of color to the otherwise white dining area, while a dramatic pop art work contrasts with the neoclassical architecture and ornate tabletop settings. As in chess, minor moves can have important consequences.

GLASS
GLAS | VERRE
CONCRETE
BETON | BÉTON
COUNTRY HOUSES
MICHELANGELO
EN PASSANT PAR LA DEMEURE

Page 183: A white-gold-colored metallic painting made of repurposed Coca-Cola cans and an English-style hurricane lamp define the entry corridor, which leads to the library.

Previous pages: An arrangement of Klimt-esque paintings by Sergey Smirnov are illuminated by a pair of French nineteenth-century candelabras and John Boone cocktail side-table lamps. Custom Christopher Hyland throw pillows bring a level of sophistication to the room.

Opposite: An 1830s Biedermeier drop-front desk serves as a pedestal for a Buddha head. The sconces are French eighteenth-century crystal candelabras.

ALEXANDER McQUEEN: SAVAGE BEAUTY

ANDO
ARCHITECTURE
INSPIRATIONS

Early Georgian Interiors
HOUSES
THE ENGLISH COUNTRY HOUSE

ATOM

Pages 188–189, from left to right: In the oak library, a cast bronze hand-chased Charles Paris lamp accents a lacquer chinoiserie hand-painted table by John Boone. A painting by Oleg Vassiliev hangs above a tufted leather sofa from George Smith; a nineteenth-century Baltic chandelier with blue glass and a pair of gilt ormolu French sconces illuminate the space. A partner's desk sits on an antique Persian rug.

Pages 190–191: A large modernist painting by Oleg Vassiliev enlivens the living room. A pair of period Louis XV chairs from Lars Bolander contrasts with an otherwise clean-lined room void of color. Simple details, such as the metal work on the mirror-top cocktail tables by John Boone and the carving on the antique French mirror above the fireplace, stand out against the simplicity of the white-painted space.

Preceding pages: A pair of large bifold glass screens bifurcate the living and dining rooms. Curtain and pillow fabrics are from Christopher Hyland and the fauteuils are nineteenth-century French.

Opposite: A dramatic contemporary pop art painting hangs above a nineteenth-century Napoleonic console.

ДОМ

Above: To the left of the master bedroom headboard niche, a paneled phantom door provides access to a large dressing room. A Sergey Smirnov portrait with a silver frame is lit by a ceramic lamp from Daniel Barney.

Opposite: A modernist artwork acts as an inspirational catalyst for an otherwise Gustavian-themed room.

The House of Tomorrow

Como

Sometimes, knowing what not to do is as important as knowing what to do. The clean lines of this apartment by Giuseppe Terragni, the pioneer of Italian rationalism and master architect of the renowned 1930s "Casa del Fascio," did not invite intervention. The challenge here was making the space warm and livable while not detracting from Terragni's somewhat severe architecture.

The apartment building, known as the "House of Tomorrow," featured original architectural elements too iconic to disrupt (though one key feature, a wooden grid, was added by the architecture and design firm Arkham Projects). The goal was to enliven the historic spaces with a few well-chosen furnishings, artwork, vibrant colors, and textures. Bold illustrative art takes cues from the apartment's sharp lines and vibrant orange-painted walls. A simple modern sectional sofa with a matching ottoman in the living room is a comfortable refuge in an otherwise spartan environment. In the dining room, a rectilinear table is coupled and contrasted with Lucite chairs and a glass pendant fixture. The bedroom is adorned only by a series of red fabric panels and a low headboard against a sconce-lit orange wall with graphically strong art by Alberto Rizzo for *Vogue*. The house of tomorrow that once made tomorrow seem forbidding, is now a historical apartment of yesteryear, and a comfortable house of today.

Page 199: Red, orange, and gray–painted walls provide a background for the dining area with art by Alberto Rizzo. A modern table and chairs create a rhythm against a polished concrete floor.

Preceding pages: A two-piece steam disc lamp and gray bowl act as accessories in an open, airy living room. Art by Alberto Rizzo hangs above a sofa sectional and matching ottoman that also functions as a coffee table.

Above: Orange-tinted plexiglass adds color to a collection of tea and coffee pots.

Opposite: A hammered Thai silver bowl sits in a modern cabinet as one enters a minimalist kitchen delineated by a shelving unit and an aluminum frame and frosted glass door.

SMEG
mou

The corridor to the mosaic-tiled bathroom is defined by a translucent shelving grid that separates it from the adjoining kitchen.

Opposite: The bathroom retains the original rationalist intention of the apartment complex, but a wood-framed niche with candles and seashells adds an organic element.

Following pages: A graphic composition by Alberto Rizzo hangs over the minimalist headboard. Red linen window panels serve as rhythmic banners providing a sense of privacy.

Gatehouse in the Hills

Como

The Lake Como area has long attracted famous visitors, from Mozart to Madonna. Its Villa d'Este, built in the sixteenth century for the Cardinal of Como, is one of Italy's most beautiful hotels. I first became familiar with this region while studying architecture in Rome, traveling around Lake Como on a custom Cinelli bicycle. Como, like the city of Chiang Mai, Thailand, where my father grew up, is known for its exquisite silks and hand-thrown pottery.

This home, part Tuscan farmhouse, part Cistercian monastery, is truly unique—a gatekeeper's farm cottage built solidly into a hillside. Unlike many of the surrounding grand villas, the building's authenticity and character had been earned by its patina—the shimmering burnished exterior of the stone can't be bought. Inside, the hand-scraped wood ceiling beams imparted both dignity and charm to the structure. But that didn't mean we couldn't introduce a few modern elements, like a simple wooden plank bookcase in the sitting room across from a centuries-old fireplace.

The living room has walls of deep cranberry red, which we chose for its warmth, with Thai silk throws and a vibrant antique Tabriz rug heightening the color scheme. The goal was to meld old-world European sophistication with an almost modern simplicity.

In the entry foyer, bare stone walls are warmed by a modest wood-burning stove and a minimalist African Bubinga wooden console containing two sunken stone bowls. Glowing objects, like a brass sleeve flue and a copper serving tray, add just enough sparkle to the otherwise serene, ascetic spaces.

Page 211: A pair of painted metal duck figures stands in front of the portal doorstops propping open the double doors.

Pages 212–213, from left to right: A 1930s Italian deco side table supports a bulbous porcelain vase whose shape is echoed in a blown hanging pendant over the stairwell; a painted wooden floor lantern and delft ceramic oven establish a sense of intrigue in the landing.

Preceding pages: A Sultanabad rug and deep Moroccan-red walls play off the simple white linen upholstered sofa and arm chair. A collection of silver boxes adorns the wooden center table.

Opposite: A pair of glass hurricane candleholders flanks a lithograph on a dramatic three-sided fireplace mantel.

SILVIO BERTOLDI
Paulo Coelho
RAFFAELLO

Preceding pages: A hard stone floor provides a smooth surface to contrast with the textures of the antler chandelier, rustic stone fireplace, and wooden plank bookcase. An Italian neoclassical center table with a porcelain tea service conveys a sense of refinement.

Opposite: A vertical copper flue adds a colorful touch of warmth in a predominantly Scandinavian-themed room. A painted Gustavian-inspired side chair rests at the window next to a nickel-plated butler's valet.

Opposite: A set of Parisian-style outdoor café chairs keeps the overall feel in the kitchen light and airy.

Above: A wood-handled skillet and a collection of quilted potholders accompany a traditional cast-iron kitchen range.

Above: In the breakfast room, a contemporary single-handed circular copper tray from Germany becomes the focal point of a nineteenth-century Italian painted wood center table.

Opposite: An assortment of handpicked fruit from the garden adds a touch of color to the table.

Opposite: Neoclassical painted armchairs designate the view to the garden terrace, where a Buddha figure sits in a state of meditative contemplation.

Above: A folding serving tray functions as a bedside table, while a pair of nineteenth-century Italian painted metal candelabras above the headboard makes for romantic evenings.

Opposite: A moss-covered stone stair sets the backdrop to the rear entrance, where time appears to have stood still since the days of the Renaissance.

Following pages: A pair of stone vessels nestles into a contemporary wooden vanity, which stands apart from the original sixteenth-century stone walls. A wood-burning stove provides warmth on a crisp early autumn day.

Pages 232–233: Nature embraces the hilltop cottage that overlooks Lake Como, reminiscent of the beauty of times past when life was perhaps less complicated.

Fornasetti Dream

Manhattan

Changes in one's physical environment can parallel—and underscore—a transformation of the inner self. My client was moving to Manhattan from Connecticut, where she raised three children in a suburban lifestyle. She had recently bought a large apartment with front and back terraces. Able to once again partake in Manhattan's cultural offerings, she was looking for a glamorous, but not flashy, environment.

A full gut renovation allowed for the creation of a gossamer master bathroom, with all white glass and frosted mirror. The client wanted that room to feel like a cloud, with the only color coming from the veining in the Calacatta marble and copper-colored fixtures and accessories. To continue the ethereal theme, the apartment was painted white and gray, with bright color residing only in the contemporary art and objects used for entertaining. The new loft-like layout of the apartment treated the kitchen as an art object in its own right, with highly lacquered dyed ebony Macassar millwork.

The client, a frequent visitor to Italy, requested that we incorporate Italian crafts, such as exotic wood and embossed leather furniture, and Venetian plaster in all the rooms. But the main traces of Italy are in the collections of antique, vintage, and contemporary glassware from Venini, Seguso, Moretti, and other Murano studios, which give the apartment jolts of color. Flanking the minimalist fireplace are two backlit niches displaying surreal Fornasetti dinnerware. There are gold-lacquered Fornasetti pieces on a striking console table below a tricolor Achille Salvagni mirror in the foyer. From each plate, the face of the operatic soprano Lina Cavalieri, Piero Fornasetti's eternal muse, peers at us, perhaps wondering why her existence is purely black and white in a world of vibrant color.

FORNASETTI
PARIS IN THE 1920s
PARIS IN THE 1920s
NEW YORK
SCULPTUR
JOURNEYS

Page 235: In the foyer a gold and gunmetal mirror by Achille Salvagni from Maison Gerard complements a pair of Parisian gold and black nickel sconces by Maison Charles. The Holly Hunt console provides a display for a set of gold-glazed Fornasetti plates.

Preceding pages: A welcoming purple and gray chair by Romeo Sozzi offers up its cast bronze arms opposite a velvet sofa by Biasi Catani. Polychromatic Fortuny pillows add color and accentuate a rug by Marc Phillips. An abstract bronze sculpture by the Thai artist Inson Wongsam sits next to a Fornasetti octopus tray.

Opposite: Refurbished mid-century chairs from Todd Merrill Studio surround a stone-topped extendable dining table from Domus Design Collection. A Lindsay Adelman chandelier floats above a dramatic Alberto Rizzo photo placed on a bronze and leather console from BDDW.

Following pages: Opposite the white lacquer master bathroom double vanity, an elegant black-and-white Fornasetti hand-painted lacquer stool completes a sea of frosted mirror.

Remembrance of Things Past

Saint-Tropez

This farmhouse, built in the late seventeenth century, appears to be untouched; it's a time capsule of life in the French countryside. And that's the way we left it—we didn't eliminate any of the building's charming imperfections. The goal was to accommodate twenty-person lunches and dinners while maintaining the house's modest demeanor. The kitchen has no upper cabinets that could interfere with the views of the garden. Upstairs windows, cut into thick walls, frame views to the orchards and the blue water of the Riviera beyond. Furniture is upholstered in natural cotton and silk linens—with only a touch of color in a throw pillow here or there. Why distract from the rotating bouquets of flowers grown in the property's expansive gardens and distributed daily throughout the house?

The entry foyer opens into a large hall leading to the spacious living room and sunlit library. The main hall, which doubles as a dining room, contains an expandable circular table that supplements the three outdoor dining areas. The clients' collection of Portuguese ceramic bowls and delftware complement the bubble glass vases and tumblers from the Alpes-Maritimes glass-blowing village of Biot.

A late-eighteenth-century French armchair accompanies an early seventeenth-century desk in the library. On the upper-level landing, a wicker chair provides a comfortable respite for leisure reading and wine sipping as the summer breeze rolls in. The home is conducive to both sleepy summers and festive dinners; when guests turn to storytelling, they sense that the house has its own story to tell too.

THE UNKNOWN MODIGLIANI
LIVING IN STYLE SCANDINAVI
CHANEL
COLETTE
Panasonic

Doré · La Bible

Page 243: A pair of nineteenth-century bronze French roosters, an antique nautical bronze bell, and a refurbished glass gas lamp greet guests at the entry door.

Pages 244–245: A pair of nineteenth-century French St. Clement bird candleholders meet with a distressed coffee table made from a repurposed workbench. An eighteenth-century Italian ceramic vessel becomes a side-table lamp, while linen throw pillows exude a summer ease.

Pages 246–247: In the library, a Chinese Kangxi-style urn turned lamp rests on an eighteenth-century French painted table used as a desk.

Pages 248–249: An early-twentieth-century carved African figural stool in the form of a bird provides a place to rest at the door to the garden dining terrace. A nineteenth-century neoclassical Italian marble case lamp graces a nineteenth-century French painted commode.

Preceding pages, from left to right: A collection of glasses from La Rochere and La Verrerie de Biot are mixed with a collection of faience porcelain from France, Italy, and Spain combined with a few assorted pieces of Dutch delft; in the kitchen, hooks on a shelf provide easy access to cooking tools. A blue linen fabric on a brass curtain rod houses a collection of copper pans below.

Opposite: Spanish and Portuguese faience becomes the focal point on a center table, while a large oversized pillow in the living room complements the turquoise porcelain.

Above: A pair of eighteenth-century porcelain bowls rests on an eighteenth-century French chest of drawers. A cast bronze sculpture by Charles Paris completes the scene.

A hand-embroidered pillow rests on a wicker chair below a circular mirror with a decorative inlay.

Opposite: A collection of sun hats acts as a decorative motif above a French Provence oak desk.

Above: An eclectic mix of contemporary modern elements contrasts with a whimsical bed crown.

Above: An arched opening provides a breathtaking view of the Mediterranean.

Opposite: A pair of niches on either side of a sunlit tub provides a place for large bouquets of flowers from the garden.

Following pages: The verdant gardens surrounding this historic home are rich with history.

Carriage House
Manhattan

Now known as the Waterfall Mansion, this former Manhattan carriage house was once a storage site for horse-drawn carriages, but these days it contains a lot of modern and contemporary art. Collectible furnishings are set against custom finishes by artisan craftsmen like Gracie, a third-generation fabricator of hand-painted wall coverings. With the various elements in harmony, the house flows as smoothly as the interior waterfall, the home's namesake and defining feature. Renovated by architect Toshiko Mori, the house had strong lines but the interiors were considered a bit austere for my client, a real estate, finance, and art world visionary.

I met her request for a more striking look by redoing the kitchen cabinets in white lacquer and ebony Macassar, dying the floors light gray, and introducing Venetian plaster accent walls and floor-to-ceiling woven-silk curtains. We incorporated furniture and accessories that could hold their own against the attention-grabbing artworks. Most of all, my team strove to avoid the monotony of pure white gallery walls; each floor landing is distinguished by its own hand-painted wallpaper. The interior waterfall remained in place—cascading down the twenty-five-foot-high back wall of the main entertainment and exhibition space—though it now serves as a setting for the work of Korean ceramicist Jae Yong Kim and an oversized hyperrealist sculpture of a swimmer by Carole Feuerman.

The challenge in the other rooms was to add luxurious touches without creating distractions. I relied on a mix of mid-century and contemporary furniture, including some oversized pieces that will "hold the floor" in any context.

As one ascends, the composition simplifies, culminating in the minimalist master bedroom and home office, where elegant silk moiré curtains flank a dramatic angled fourteen-by-twenty-foot window. Light floods onto an organic natural-edge desk by John Houshmand, which contrasts with the otherwise modern aesthetic. Within the context of this house, Houshmand, formerly a builder, is a craftsman and I, an architecturally trained designer, become an aesthetically driven curator. Among the overwhelming abundance of art, the lines between disciplines blur.

Gehry
Frank O.
Gehry
FIREFLY

PHAIDON ATLAS
CONTEMPORARY WORLD ARCHITECTURE

Page 263: A Carole Feuerman sculpture borders the edge of a reflecting pool at the bottom of a thirty-foot waterfall.

Preceding pages: A sculpture by British-born artist Venetia Walkey highlights a Romeo Sozzi coffee table. An oversized Hervé Van Der Straeten chandelier floats over an aquamarine contemporary carpet from Doris Leslie Blau.

Opposite: In the dressing room, a colorful modern sculpture and a dynamic tapestry serving as a floor covering are juxtaposed with a clean-lined Italian mid-century Murano glass lamp and table by John Houshmand.

STOCKMAN

CHANEL CHANEL CHANEL CHANEL
HERMÈS PARIS
HERMÈS PARIS
YVES SAINT LAURENT
VOGUE

Preceding pages: Designer Drugs by artist Jonathan Paul of Desire Obtain Cherish hangs above an acrylic wood mold cast table and chairs by John Houshmand. Fabric from Donghia forms the window treatments.

Opposite: A John Houshmand table pairs with a rug by Marc Phillips.

Above: A glass table with a singular horizontal wooden beam acts as a conceptual anchor to the bed, which floats against a glass window with the Manhattan skyline as its headboard.

Opposite: A painting by Marcello Lo Giudice from Unix Gallery brings out the red in a rug by Marc Phillips.

A 1968 black-and-white photo by Alberto Rizzo for *Vogue Italia* sits above a wooden screen that was transformed into a headboard. A metal table by John Lyle and a Poltrona Frau chair complete the room.

THE WORLD IN VOGUE PEOPLE PARTIES PLACES

Almond Orchard

Mallorca

After I completed their Greenwich, Connecticut, mansion, my clients asked me to help finish a villa they were building near Satanyí, Mallorca—one of my favorite places in the world.

I had no idea what a spectacular project this was until I drove up a dusty, unnamed farm road onto a long driveway that snaked through miles of fragrant almond orchards. This three-story hilltop house, with distant views of the Mediterranean, was built entirely of French limestone in classic Palladian proportions. Inside, rustic stone floors, plaster moldings, and high ceilings suggested a manor house from days gone by.

The contemporary house creates connections between interior and exterior spaces. Directly behind the entry foyer is a striking terrace bordered by flowers and a lush vine-engulfed trellis. To capitalize on the view of the inviting outdoor space, we designed a kitchen and breakfast area behind a wall of glass. Inside the kitchen, a large farm table was set right against the island to encourage guests to interact with their hosts and taste-test during the convivial preparation of meals.

The owners asked me to incorporate some antiques they already owned, mostly from Catalonia and the South of France. To those we added elements not originally intended as design objects: an old barn door, hand-scraped by local workers, became a coffee table; a farm hat and fabulous vintage wine jug found at the local market became accent pieces. This layering of old and new helped create the feeling that the house had been lived in for generations. We made sure the rooms looked relaxed and unfussy. Unmatched pieces were placed casually, rather than in careful, symmetrical groupings.

In the master bedroom, where serenity is paramount, we avoided anything superfluous. The walls, carpet, bed, daybed, and sofas are all rendered in a neutral, all-natural linen. In the main areas, we were bolder: the Moroccan carpet in the living room is a deep burgundy, like the local wine. We wanted to capture the feeling of siestas and sangrias. With peaceful bedrooms upstairs and an expansive dining area with an accommodating bar downstairs, the scene is set to relax with friends.

museu art modern contemporani de palma

MALLORCA
JOAN BENNÀSSAR

Page 277: The stair to the upper master wing has marble treads that contrast with the simple limestone floors of the entry foyer.

Pages 278–279: A Mediterranean palette in the living room cultivates a relaxed atmosphere.

Preceding pages: Nautical-themed accessories, repurposed antique doors, and wooden antiques purchased in Barcelona warm the living room and echo the surrounding land.

Opposite: In close proximity to the kitchen, the dining area provides an informal and flexible environment.

Above: The master bedroom has decorative elements from local villages mixed with finds from trips to Africa and Asia.

Opposite: A wrought iron Spanish candelabra finishes the metal headboard, which has been softened by a Thai silk scarf.

Preceding pages: With an abundance of flowers mixed with antiques and found objects, the outdoor covered terrace invites a sense of relaxation.

Opposite: An overturned antique terra-cotta jar radiates the laissez-faire attitude of the people who inhabit the utopian island of Mallorca.

White on White

New York

Can the same person inhabit two environments, or does a different environment invariably change a person? My client, who owns a large house in Boca Raton, Florida, also bought a New York studio to use as a pied-à-terre. Here, the goal was to achieve a Zen-like outlook—to leave the complications of the city behind. Although the building had been recently renovated, the developer's finishes were not calming. (Plus, there were practical problems, like a lack of storage space, that had to be resolved.) The design evolved out of a strategy of composition by absence—removing all color and hiding nearly everything utilitarian. White lacquered built-ins conceal a Murphy bed and large flat-screen TV. On the floor, crystalline white glass was used to create a tabula rasa. A thick, heavily textured white leather sectional placed on a pure silk high-pile rug exudes confidence and asserts and embeds itself in its crystal environment.

The room that best displays its minimalist leanings is the kitchen. Custom stainless-steel cabinets levitate above an island covered in two-inch-thick cast white glass. Of course, with so little visual camouflage, even the smallest details matter. Here, the countertops are aligned down to a fraction of a millimeter with the edge of the drawers, producing a pure ninety-degree edge precisely lined up with the stainless steel. Even the bathroom and walk-in closet are clad in white glass (partitioned only by frosted mirrors). The effect is to let the inhabitant—my philanthropically minded client—meditate on nothingness. If, as Mies van der Rohe said, "God is in the details," this space is ideal for a moment of reflection void of distractions.

Page 291: A customized Eero Saarinen table and white glass floors are warmed by a single parchment-topped mid-century modern curved wood bench.

Preceding pages: Bronze sconces by Charles Paris act as sculptures in a monochromatic environment, where their organic shape stands apart.

Opposite: The kitchen has a combination of streamlined stainless steel with two-inch-thick white glass countertops. An Alison Berger crystal pendant sits over an island filled with rollout drawers. Window jambs and the backsplash have been lined with frosted mirror that complements the stainless steel.

Statuesque

Saint-Tropez

This Italian-influenced seventeenth-century structure is located just outside of Saint-Tropez, a place so convivial that the weather is always set to room temperature. The owner, a retired architect, treated the house as an archeological find—its beauty to be revealed, not disturbed.

Within the old envelope, modern and antique pieces were woven together to make the space simultaneously livable and unstudied. A carved stone sink, the focal point of the kitchen, conjures a cross between the baroque master Francesco Borromini and the expressive modernist Carlo Scarpa, and sits beneath circular, nautical-inspired windows.

Touches of streamlined mid-century modern and French Provençal furniture balance out the original heavy masonry walls. Paper cutouts of Roman emperor busts sit on wooden pedestals and whimsically reference the era when a man's home was his castle. A vibrant yellow ceramic dog casually rests on a bright red coffee table to invoke more levity. As sunbeams refract through deep, open windows, the environment lulls us into adaptive repose. Whatever daily challenges we endure have flown away—leaving just a patterned heartbeat echoing with the sound of the ocean.

Page 297: An arched doorway frames a French plaster sculpture of Aphrodite (Venus in Roman mythology), the goddess of love and beauty, which is reminiscent of Jean-Antoine Houdon's 1782 work, *Baigneuse.*

Preceding pages: An eclectic mix of styles defines the living room, which features linen-covered sofas around a cocktail table with an antique French marble top standing on a base made of two large ceramic vases turned upside down. The mantel doubles as a secondary frame for a painting and as a pedestal for an array of decorative objects.

Above: A collection of porcelain vases adorns a painted French wooden console.

Opposite: A Roman emperor cutout sitting on an oval-shaped wooden storage cabinet pedestal serves as a whimsical backdrop and place to display family photos and childhood collectibles.

WATTEAU
DEMEURES DE SICILE
INTERIORS

Opposite: A faux-marble-painted wooden column base supporting a stone top makes for an innovative desk. A collection of large ocean liner models conveys the owner's love for nautical themes and adds color.

Above: A Carlo Bugatti–inspired floor lamp accompanies a hand sketch of a nude applied directly to the plaster stucco wall. A collection of art objects pairs with a battleship display.

Following pages: A retractable sliding door provides an abundance of light, which floods the sitting room with vibrant colors. The rough exterior stucco wall contrasts nicely against the highly polished 1950s red lacquer table, yellow ceramic dog, and polished nickel bowl.

FORTNUM & MASON
Spice Importers
TEA DEALERS &
GROCERS

Preceding pages: A carved stone double sink in the kitchen, evoking Francesco Borromini's Renaissance fountain at San Carlo alle Quattro Fontane, provides an inspiring place for preparing culinary delights. Nautical-inspired windows offer views to the garden.

Opposite: A series of stone and inlay obelisks point to a drawing of a nineteenth-century architecture pavilion. Paintings and books casually lie on the floor under a hand-carved eighteenth-century wooden console table.

Mirrored, limed, and cerused double French doors open onto the bedroom, which is accentuated with a modest canopy and a French period Louis XVI walnut bench.

Opposite: Repurposed antique medallions inserted in the bathtub enclosure add intrigue and emphasize the owner's love for neoclassical architecture. An arched dome above the bath frames a view of the oval window to the gardens outside.

Following pages, from left to right: In the garden, a sculpture of a muscular bull reminds us of the agrarian heritage of the South of France; the roof terrace affords breathtaking vistas of the Mediterranean.

Pages 316–317: The simple, symmetrical pool frames a sculpture of Venus entering her bath inspired by Christophe-Gabriel Allegrain's *Baigneuse* at the Louvre.

Pages 319: A decorative diamond necklace hangs around the neck of Venus, reminding viewers of the beauty of life's impermanence . . . or the permanence of life's beauty.

Acknowledgments

Thank you to my clients for allowing me to share their beautiful homes and for believing in my vision. I am grateful to them for taking this journey with me in what can sometimes be an all-consuming endeavor. Without them, this book would not exist.

I want to thank Mark Roskams for his phenomenal photography, resiliency, and ability to work under trying conditions. He beautifully captured the true essence of each project. Thanks is owed to Cristina Rizzo for orchestrating these 320 pages of wonderment: like a film director, she coordinated crews on three continents, staged interiors, and synthesized diverse images into a moving visual experience. Her patience and keen editor's eye imbue every photo. Similarly, the sharp instincts and unique eye of George Foreman helped facilitate production from beginning to end.

I would like to thank the vendors, contractors, employees, and interns who have worked with me, past and present. Luckily, while I'm teaching them, they're teaching me.

I've also benefited from the instruction of past mentors, such as Juan-Pablo Molyneux and David Easton. To each person who has employed and challenged me, I am forever grateful.

With the utmost respect for Charles Miers and my editor, Daniel Melamud, a debt of gratitude for their countless hours of polishing this monograph, and to the entire Rizzoli team as well as the book's designer, Geoffrey Dunne, for an incredible job. Without their attention to detail, both visual and literary, this book would not be of the same caliber.

Thank you to my friends, family, and partner, Elba. A special thanks to Judith Rifkin, who helped organize my thoughts and edit my words.

Last, but not least, a debt of kindness is owed to all the people in our travels who have welcomed us and made us feel truly part of a global and inviting village.

First published in the United States of America in 2016
by Rizzoli International Publications, Inc.
300 Park Avenue South
New York, NY 10010
www.rizzoliusa.com

Edited by Daniel Melamud and Cristina Rizzo
Design: Geoffrey Dunne
Production: Susan Lynch
Copy editing: Victorine Lamothe-Maurin
Proofreading: Elizabeth Smith

Library of Congress Control Number: 2016940219
ISBN-13: 978-0-8478-4873-7

2016 2017 2018 2019 / 10 9 8 7 6 5 4 3 2 1
Printed in China